Floating Boats

Frances Ridley

OXFORD
UNIVERSITY PRESS

Let's make boats!

Will this float?

3

We put a bowl in the water.

4

Will these float?
marbles

We put some marbles in the water.

No, they sink.

Put them on this!

We put some marbles in the bowl.

8

Will this float?
clay ball

We put a clay ball in the water.

We made a clay boat.

We put the clay boat in the water.

We made two boats!
What did we put in them?

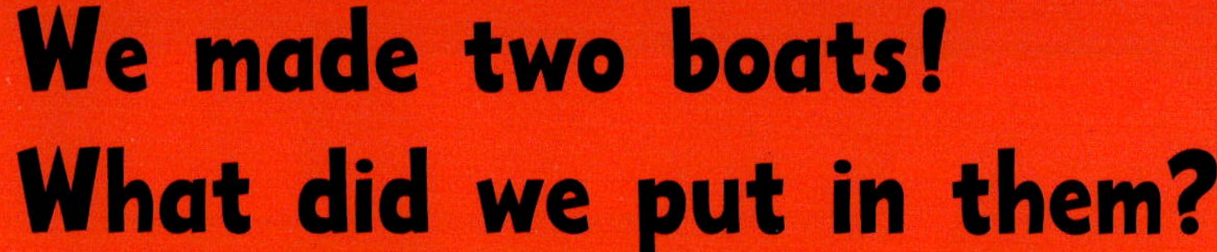

Can you make a boat?

Try these things.

Write it down like this.